SMILE
THE WISDOM OF
Joy

SMILE
THE WISDOM OF

Joy

AFFIRMATIONS AND QUOTATIONS TO INSPIRE HAPPINESS

CICO BOOKS
LONDON · NEW YORK

Published in 2022 by CICO Books
An imprint of Ryland Peters & Small Ltd

20–21 Jockey's Fields
London WC1R 4BW

341 E 116th St
New York, NY 10029

www.rylandpeters.com

10 9 8 7 6 5 4 3 2 1

A CIP catalog record for this book is available from the Library
of Congress and the British Library.

ISBN: 978-1-80065-160-9

Printed in China

Designer: Louise Leffler
Commissioning editor: Kristine Pidkameny
Publishing manager: Carmel Edmonds
Art director: Sally Powell
Creative director: Leslie Harrington
Head of production: Patricia Harrington

INTRODUCTION

A smile is worth a thousand words and is capable of spreading the simple wisdom of joy. Did you know that smiling can improve our health, and the more we smile, the happier we are—and so are those around us? So much depends on our attitude and how we look at life. Joy is an inside job and we get to choose to experience it, whether alone in quiet moments of awe or surrounded by community with sharing and laughter. From its whispers that are ever present to savoring the freedom and connection it offers, joy renews and restores.

This stunning collection of life-affirming messages and images captures feelings of delight and well-being to discover the joy, hope, and vitality readily available every day. Be transported when you start or end your day, or read at times when you need a little pick-me-up. Be reminded of the many ways to experience joy daily—through pleasure, nature, humor, home life, solitude, people, acceptance, creativity, generosity, gratitude, kindness... the list is endless.

Something wonderful is about to happen.
The joyful possibilities await.
Are you ready?

A smile recures the
wounding of a frown.

William Shakespeare

Where words fail, music speaks.

Hans Christian Andersen

DISCOVER
YOUR
JOY

They might not need me;
but they might.
I'll let my head be just in sight;
a smile as small as mine might be
precisely their necessity.

Emily Dickinson

Happiness is the absence of the striving for happiness.

Chuang Tzu

Hope smiles from the threshold of the year to come, whispering, "It will be happier."

Alfred, Lord Tennyson

JOY IS NOT IN THINGS; IT IS IN US.

Richard Wagner

Be happy for no reason

*In the sweetness of friendship
let there be laughter
and sharing of pleasures.
For in the dew of little things
the heart finds its morning
and is refreshed.*

Kahlil Gibran

BLUE COLOR IS
EVERLASTINGLY
APPOINTED BY
THE DEITY TO
BE A SOURCE
OF DELIGHT.

John Ruskin

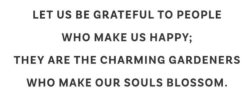

LET US BE GRATEFUL TO PEOPLE

WHO MAKE US HAPPY;

THEY ARE THE CHARMING GARDENERS

WHO MAKE OUR SOULS BLOSSOM.

Marcel Proust

All who joy would win must share it.
Happiness was born a twin.

Lord Byron

Bright blessings
shine on

A
smile
shortens
the
distance.

French proverb

SCATTER JOY!

Ralph Waldo Emerson

Capture the playful moments

There is little that separates humans from other sentient beings—we all feel joy, we all deeply crave to be alive and to live freely, and we all share this planet together.

Mahatma Gandhi

Find
joy
in
the
present
moment

TO GET THE FULL VALUE OF JOY, YOU MUST
HAVE SOMEONE TO DIVIDE IT WITH.

Mark Twain

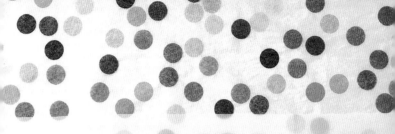

There is nothing in the
world so irresistibly
contagious as laughter
and good humor.

Charles Dickens

WITH AN EYE MADE
QUIET BY THE POWER
OF HARMONY,
AND THE DEEP
POWER OF JOY,
WE SEE INTO
THE LIFE OF THINGS.

William Wordsworth

Be comforted,
dear soul!
There is always
light behind
the clouds.

Louisa May Alcott

Friendship improves happiness and abates misery, by the doubling of our joy and the dividing of our grief.

Marcus Cicero

Gratitude

Keep on knocking,
and the joy
that is inside you
will find a window
and look out to see
who is there.

Rumi

Use your smile to change the world; don't let the world change your smile.

Chinese proverb

Wonder
when you
wander

Find ecstasy in life; the mere sense of living is joy enough.

Emily Dickinson

BEAUTY IS WHATEVER GIVES JOY.

Edna St. Vincent Millay

Welcome delight

IN DIFFICULT TIMES, CARRY SOMETHING BEAUTIFUL IN YOUR HEART

Blaise Pascal

A KIND HEART IS
A FOUNTAIN OF
GLADNESS, MAKING
EVERYTHING IN ITS
VICINITY FRESHEN
INTO SMILES.

Washington Irving

Be thou the rainbow to the storms of life!
The evening beam that smiles the cloud away,
And tints to-morrow with prophetic ray!

Lord Byron

THE PAIN OF PARTING IS NOTHING TO THE JOY OF MEETING AGAIN.

Charles Dickens

Love

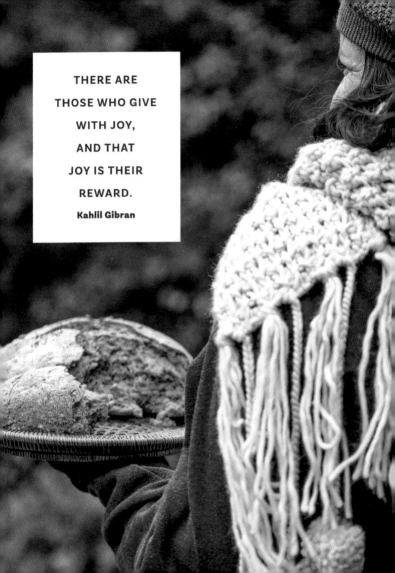

THERE ARE
THOSE WHO GIVE
WITH JOY,
AND THAT
JOY IS THEIR
REWARD.

Kahlil Gibran

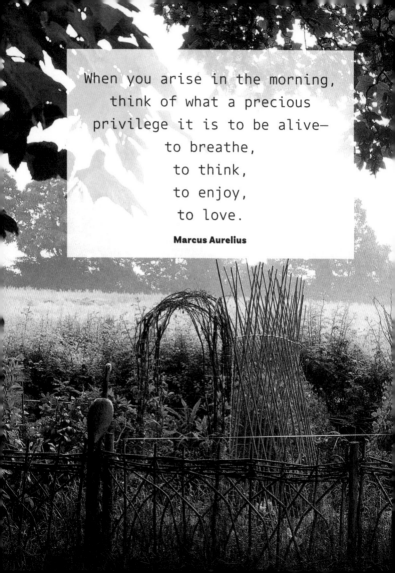

When you arise in the morning,
think of what a precious
privilege it is to be alive—
to breathe,
to think,
to enjoy,
to love.

Marcus Aurelius

With freedom,
books, flowers,
and the moon,
who could not
be happy?

Oscar Wilde

PLANT KINDNESS AND SPREAD JOY

THE SUN DOES NOT SHINE FOR A FEW TREES AND FLOWERS,
BUT FOR THE WIDE WORLD'S JOY.

Henry Ward Beecher

Health, contentment, and trust are your greatest
possessions. And freedom your greatest joy.

Buddha

THE POWER OF
FINDING BEAUTY
IN THE HUMBLEST
THINGS MAKES
HOME HAPPY AND
LIFE LOVELY.

Louisa May Alcott

Live life when you have it.
Life is a splendid gift—there
is nothing small about it.

Florence Nightingale

Make a wish

Invite the new day with a smile

NOW I REALLY FEEL THE LANDSCAPE. I CAN BE BOLD
AND INCLUDE EVERY TONE OF PINK AND BLUE:
IT'S ENCHANTING, IT'S DELICIOUS.

Claude Monet

HAPPINESS IS A HABIT—CULTIVATE IT.

Elbert Hubbard

FOLLOW YOUR JOY

Go confidently in the direction
of your dreams.

Henry David Thoreau

*Happiness is not a state
to arrive at, rather,
a manner of traveling.*

Samuel Johnson

LEARN SOMETHING NEW

Remain curious

KNOWLEDGE COMES, BUT WISDOM LINGERS.

Alfred, Lord Tennyson

Wonder
is the
beginning
of wisdom.

Socrates

THE JOY OF QUIET

If you
want
to be
happy,
be.

Leo Tolstoy

The richness
I achieve
comes from nature,
the source
of my
inspiration.

Claude Monet

ATTEND
TO
MATTERS
OF
THE
HEART

IT'S SO NICE
TO BE A SPOKE
IN THE WHEEL,
ONE THAT HELPS
TO TURN, NOT ONE
THAT HINDERS.

Gertrude Bell

NOW AND THEN IT'S GOOD TO PAUSE IN OUR PURSUIT OF HAPPINESS AND JUST BE HAPPY.

Guillaume Apollinaire

I KNOW THE JOY OF FISHES IN THE RIVER THROUGH MY OWN JO
AS I GO WALKING ALONG THE SAME RIVER.

Chuang Tzu

THE WATERFALL WINKS AT EVERY PASSERBY

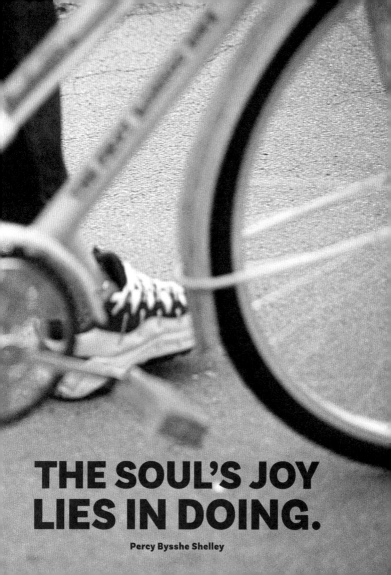

THE SOUL'S JOY LIES IN DOING.

Percy Bysshe Shelley

I have just dropped into the very place I have been seeking, but in everything it exceeds all my dreams.

Isabella Bird

Never underestimate the
healing effects of beauty.

Florence Nightingale

TODAY,
I
CHOOSE
JOY

BE HAPPY FOR THIS MOMENT: THIS MOMENT IS YOUR LIFE.

Omar Khayyam

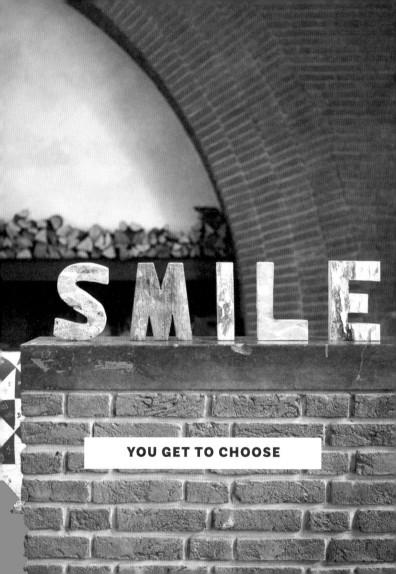

SMILE

YOU GET TO CHOOSE

Open your heart and let joy in

TAKE A BREATH
OF THE NEW DAWN
AND MAKE IT
A PART OF YOU.
IT WILL GIVE
YOU STRENGTH.

Hopi proverb

THE DOOR TO HAPPINESS OPENS OUTWARD.

Søren Kierkegaard

The joy of kindness for yourself and others

FRIENDS
ARE
THE
SUNSHINE
OF
LIFE.
John Hay

Live, and be happy, and make others so.

Mary Wollstonecraft Shelley

EXPLORE

ADVENTURE IS WORTHWHILE.

Aesop

MAKE UP YOUR MIND
TO BE HAPPY.
LEARN TO FIND PLEASURE
IN SIMPLE THINGS.

Robert Louis Stevenson

TAKE

TIME

FOR

DREAMING

A smile is the same as sunshine; it banishes
winter from the human countenance.

Victor Hugo

WHATEVER LIFTS THE CORNERS
OF YOUR MOUTH, TRUST THAT.

Rumi

The human race has one
really effective weapon,
and that is laughter.

Mark Twain

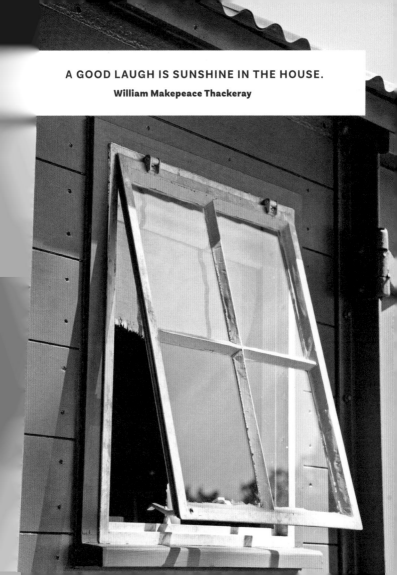

A GOOD LAUGH IS SUNSHINE IN THE HOUSE.

William Makepeace Thackeray

Share the joy

HAPPINESS DEPENDS UPON OURSELVES.   **Aristotle**

Be fascinated

JUST LIVING IS NOT ENOUGH...
ONE MUST HAVE SUNSHINE, FREEDOM,
AND A LITTLE FLOWER.

Hans Christian Andersen

EARTH LAUGHS IN FLOWERS.

Ralph Waldo Emerson

When you do things
from your soul, you
feel a river moving
in you, a joy.

Rumi

RIDE THE WAVE OF JOY

THE ART OF ART,
THE GLORY OF EXPRESSION,
IS SIMPLICITY.

Walt Whitman

HAPPINESS
IN LIFE
DEPENDS ON
VERY FEW
THINGS.

Marcus Aurelius

CONSIDER THE POSSIBILITIES

WRITE IT ON YOUR HEART THAT EVERY DAY
IS THE BEST DAY IN THE YEAR.

Ralph Waldo Emerson

What we plant in the soil of contemplation,
we shall reap in the harvest of action.

Meister Eckhart

WHEN YOU FEEL
A PEACEFUL JOY,
THAT'S WHEN
YOU ARE NEAR
TRUTH.

Rumi

THE
JOY OF
THE OPEN
ROAD

A thing of beauty
is a joy forever:
its loveliness increases;
it will never pass into
nothingness.

John Keats

Spark joy.
There's always enough to go around.

When it is dark enough, you can see the stars.

Ralph Waldo Emerson

Imagine

Dream

Wonder

LOOK UP AND FIND THE JOY

THE NOBLEST PLEASURE IS THE JOY OF UNDERSTANDING.

Leonardo da Vinci

Trouble knocked at the door,
but, hearing laughter,
hurried away.

Benjamin Franklin

Invite   Gather   Welcome

Nature's bounty

The past, the present, and the future
are really one: they are today.

Harriet Beecher Stowe

ONE MUST NEVER LOOK FOR HAPPINESS:

ONE MEETS IT BY THE WAY.

Isabelle Eberhardt

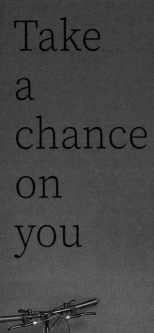

Take
a
chance
on
you

YOU MATTER

Happiness,
not in another place
but this place…
not for another hour,
but this hour.

Walt Whitman

The joy of giving

When the green woods
laugh with the voice of joy,
And the dimpling stream
runs laughing by;
When the air does laugh
with our merry wit,
And the green hill laughs
with the noise of it.

William Blake

A joy shared is a joy doubled.

Johann Wolfgang von Goethe

FIND

THE

JOY

WITHIN

Drink deeply.
Live in serenity
and joy.

Buddha

OH, THE SUMMER NIGHT, HAS A SMILE OF LIGHT,

AND SHE SITS ON A SAPPHIRE THRONE.

Bryan Procter

LOOKING FORWARD

Picture Credits

Helen Cathcart: p. 24

Holly Jolliffe: pp. 52, 72

James Fennell: pp. 68, 93

James Merrell: pp. 44, 128, 135

Jan Baldwin: pp. 35, 57, 134

Jeanette Lunde: p. 127

Joanna Henderson: pp. 28, 74, 76

Kate Whitaker: p. 129

Katrine Martensen-Larsen: p. 118

Lucinda Symons: pp. 81, 85

Mark Lohman: pp. 119, 120, 121

Mark Scott: pp. 140, 141

Martin Brigdale: pp. 122

Mowie Kay: p. 138

Paul Massey: pp. 26, 56, 77, 96

Penny Wincer: p. 20

Peter Cassidy: pp. 45, 47, 58-59, 61, 62, 92, 115, 142

Polly Wreford: pp. 7, 13, 36-37, 39, 40, 86, 112, 126

Rachel Whiting: pp. 64-65, 88, 102, 114

Richard Jung: p. 123

Sandra Lane: p. 22

Simon Brown: pp. 15, 53, 103

Steve Painter: p. 80

Tara Fisher: p. 29